D1146031

Purple Ronnie's
Little Guide to
GIRLS

by Purple Ronnie

First published 2000 by Boxtree
an imprint of Macmillan Publishers Ltd
25 Eccleston Place London SW1W 9NF
Basingstoke and Oxford

www.macmillan.co.uk

Associated companies throughout the world

ISBN 0 7522 7241 1

9 8 7 6 5 4 3 2 1

A CIP catalogue record for this book is
available from the British Library

Text by Giles Andreae
Illustrations by Janet Cronin
Printed and Bound in Hong Kong

a girl →

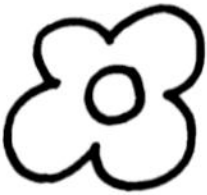

Hippy Chicks

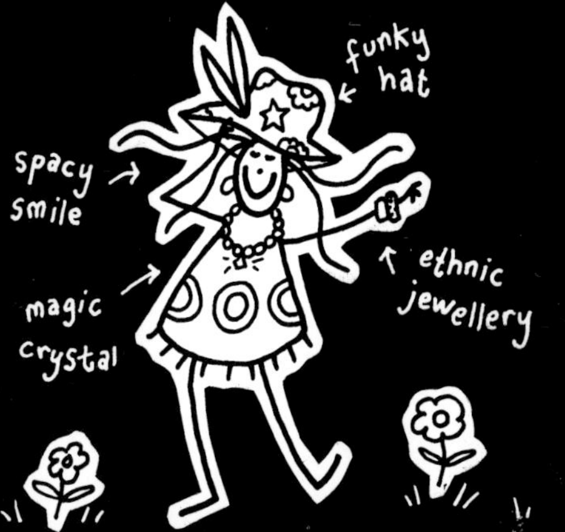
funky hat
spacy smile
ethnic jewellery
magic crystal

a poem about
↓

Hippy Chicks

They paint their nails
with love hearts

And put flowers on their
cars

And they like to boogie
naked

Underneath the stars

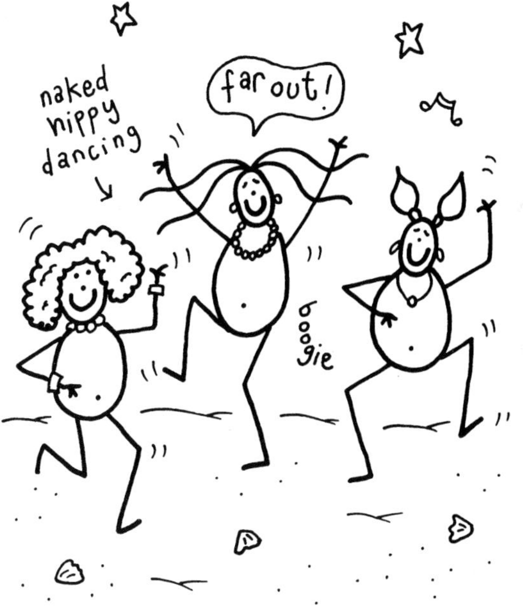
naked
nippy
dancing
far out!
boogie

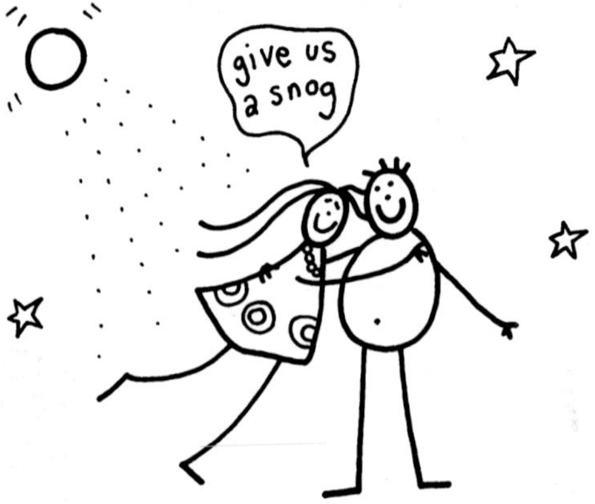
give us a snog

The moon always makes Hippy Chicks feel incredibly sexy

Girly Girls

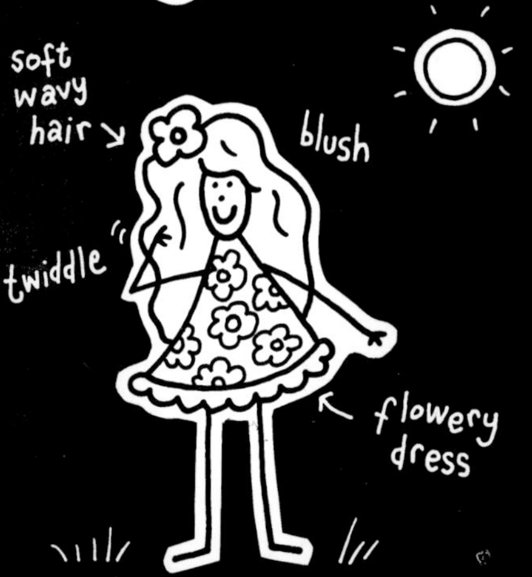

a poem about
↓

Girly Girls

Girly girls are lovely

But one snog might be
enough

Cos their lips are made
of sugar

But their brains are
made of fluff

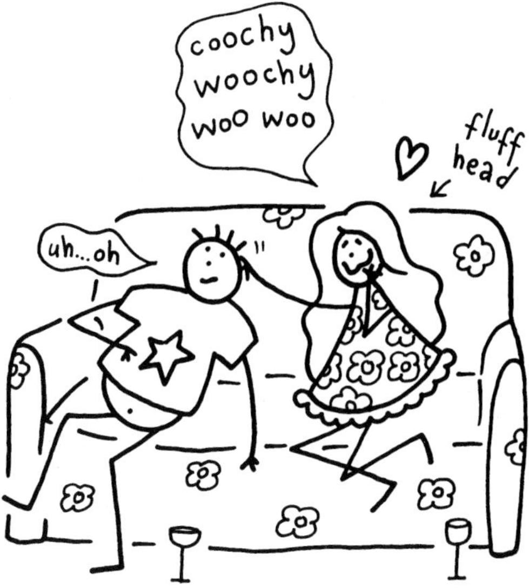
coochy woochy woo woo
fluff head
uh...oh

There is nothing a Girly Girl loves more than watching a good weepy movie on the telly

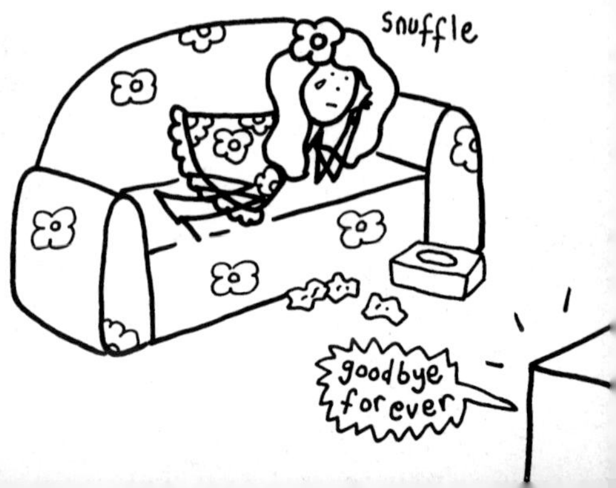
snuffle
goodbye forever

Sex Goddesses

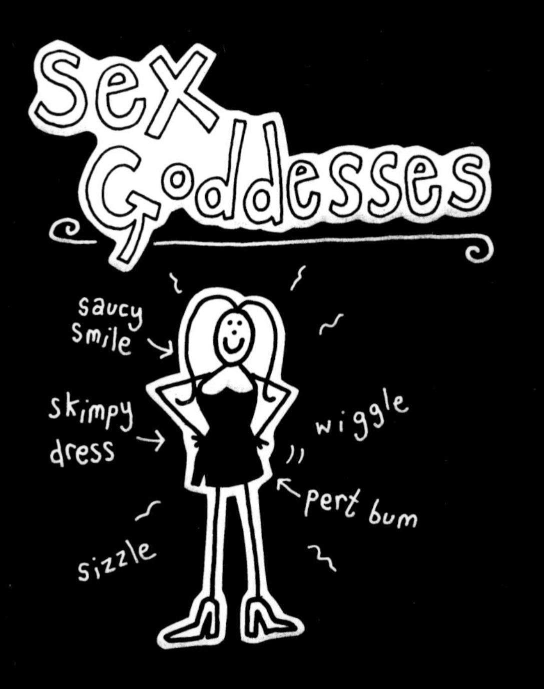
saucy smile
skimpy dress
wiggle
pert bum
sizzle

a poem about
↓
Sex Goddesses

They pout at themselves
in the mirror

To get into Sex Goddess mode

Then wink at the boys who
walk past them

And smile as their
trousers explode

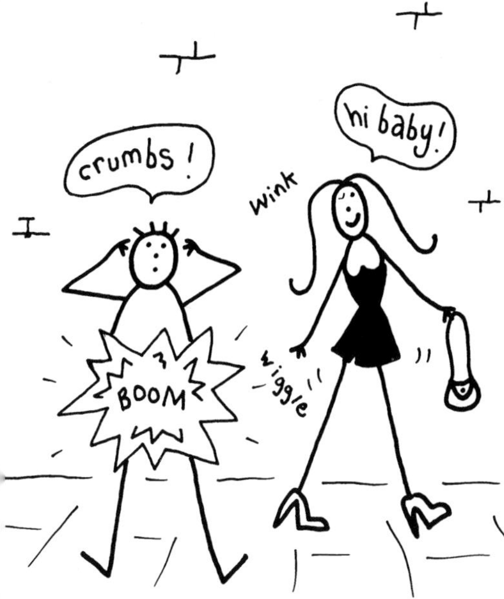
crumbs!
hi baby!
wink
BOOM
wiggle

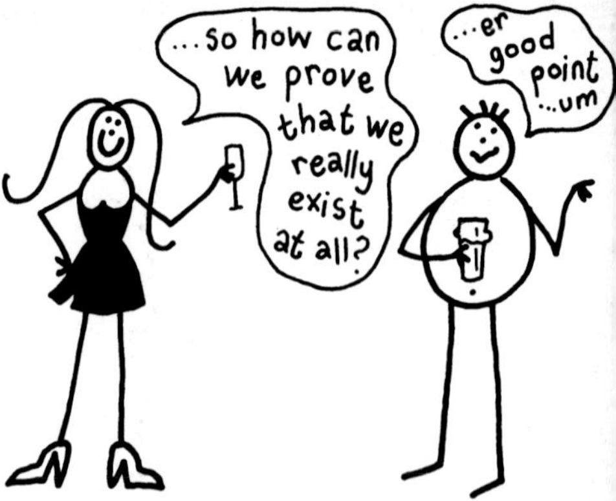
...so how can we prove that we really exist at all?
...er good point ...um

Sex Goddesses often try to talk about brainy things in case you only fancy them for their looks

Posh Girls

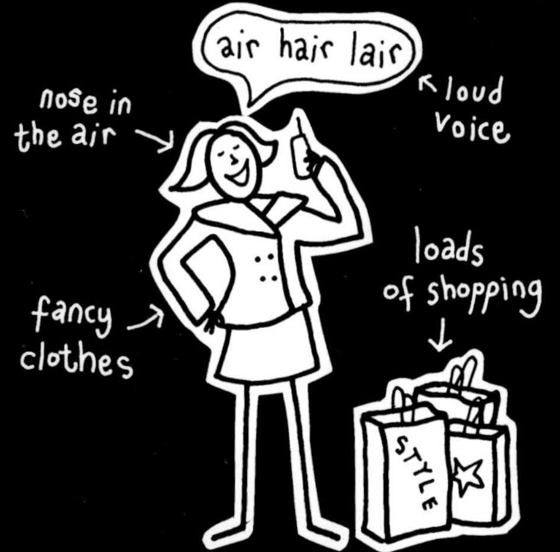
air hair lair
nose in the air
loud voice
loads of shopping
fancy clothes
STYLE

a poem about

Posh Girls

No matter where they
come from
They always talk the same
And they like to give
each other
A very silly name

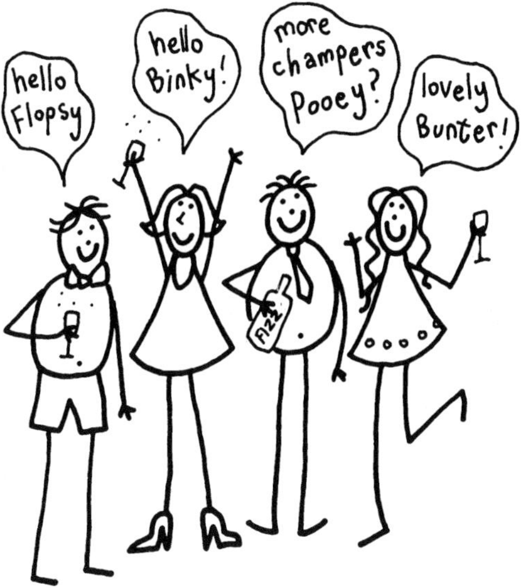
hello Flopsy
hello Binky!
more champers Pooey?
lovely Bunter!
FIZZ

When it comes to Doing It Posh Girls can sometimes have rather strange fantasies

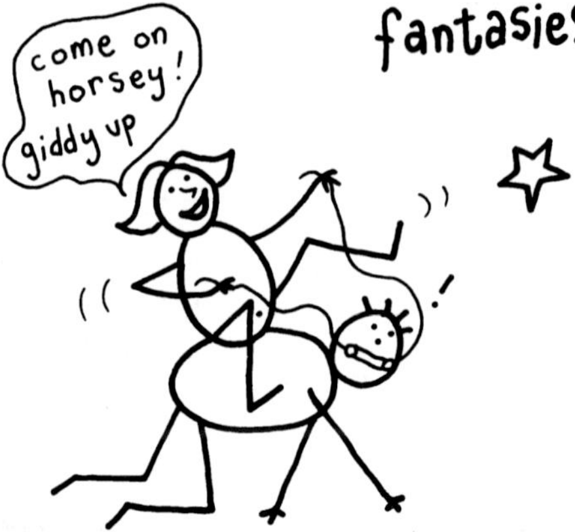
come on horsey! giddy up

Earth Mothers

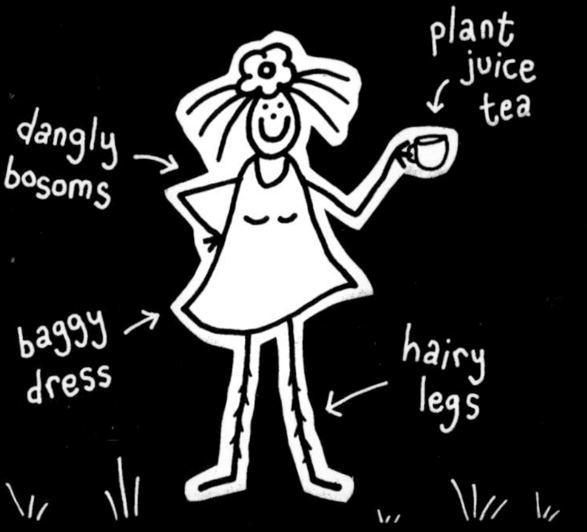
plant juice tea
dangly bosoms
baggy dress
hairy legs

a poem about

Earth Mothers

They love having baths in
rhinoceros dung
And rubbing their bosoms
with clay
It may not look pretty
Or smell very nice
But it's just much
more natural that way

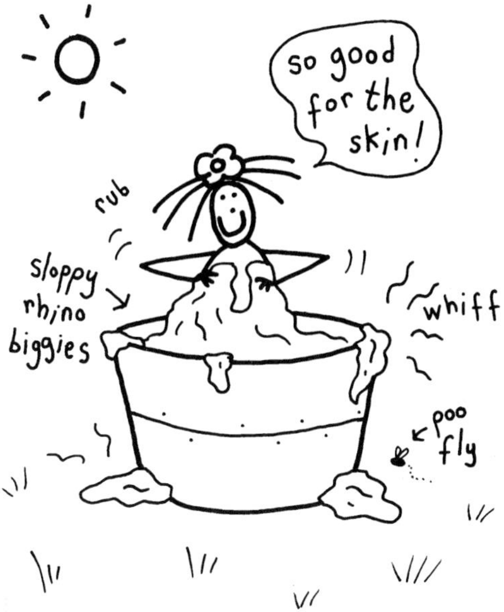
so good for the skin!
rub
sloppy rhino biggies
whiff
poo fly

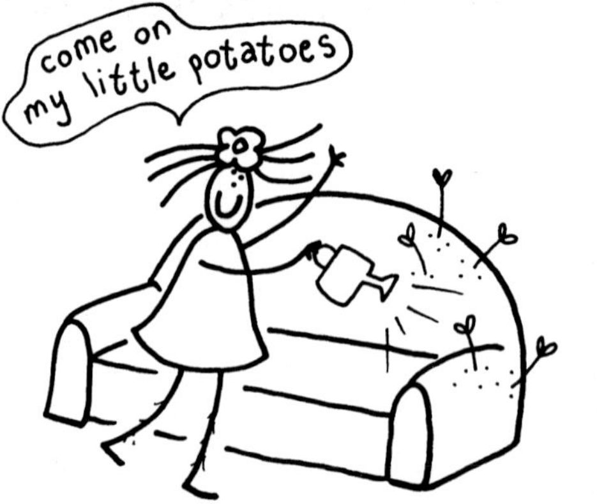
come on
my little potatoes

Earth Mothers do not need jobs because they can grow everything they need at home

Ladettes

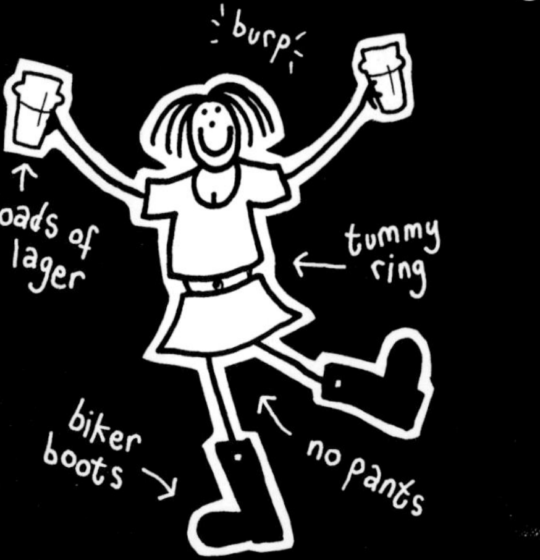
burp
loads of lager
tummy ring
biker boots
no pants

a poem about

Ladettes

Dating Ladettes is quite
frightening
Because they are easily able
To gobble hot curries
Drink twenty-five pints
And then nail your knob
to the table

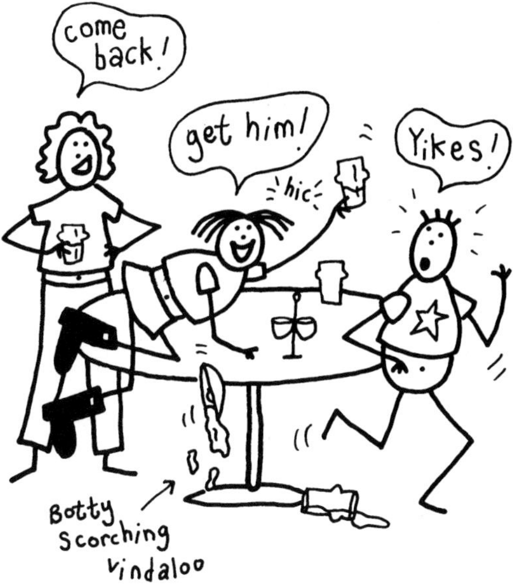
come back!
get him!
hic
Yikes!
Botty Scorching vindaloo

Ladettes believe in Girl Power, and they think most men are boring

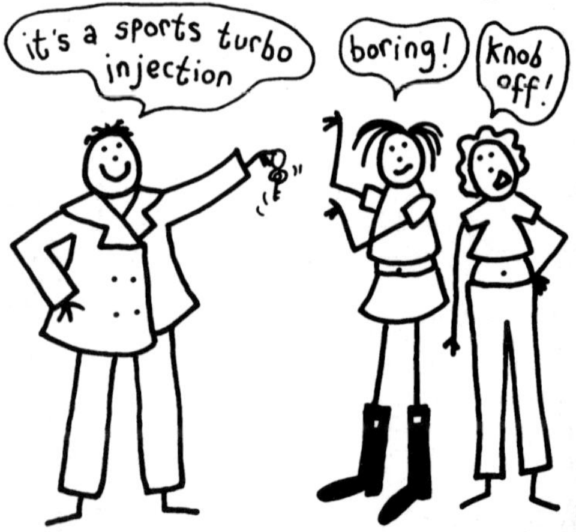
it's a sports turbo injection
boring!
Knob off!

Fashion Girls

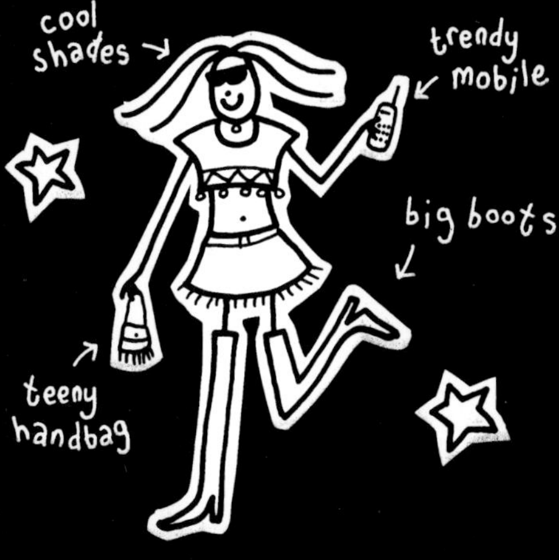
cool shades
trendy mobile
big boots
teeny handbag

a poem about ↓

Fashion Girls

If you date a fashion
girl
Your social life just stops
Cos you'll be spending
every weekend
Being dragged around
the shops

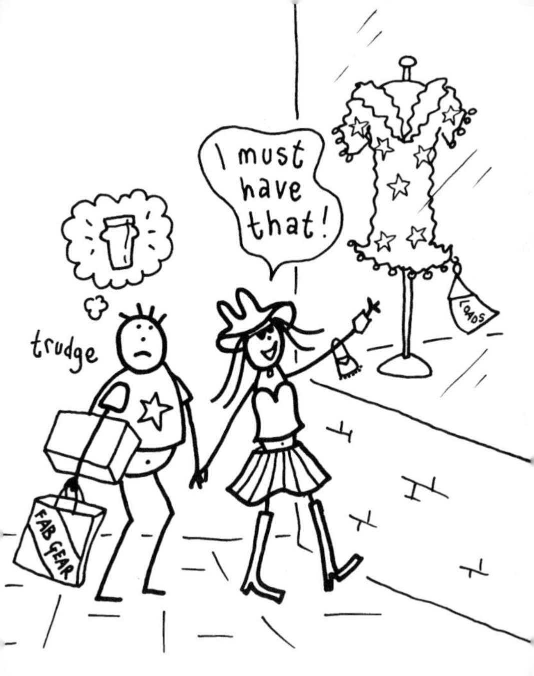
I must have that!
trudge
FAB GEAR
LOADS

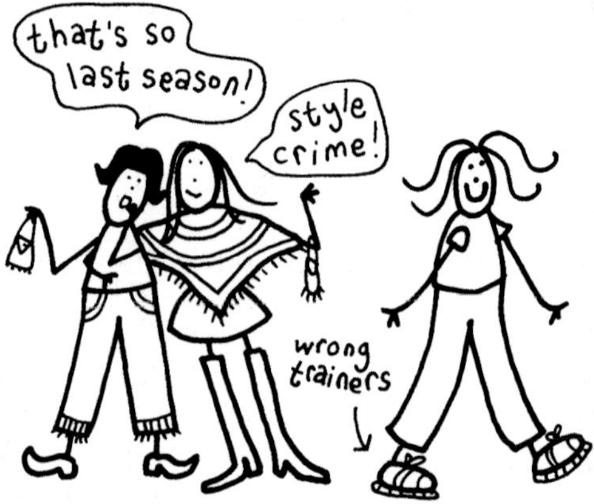
that's so last season!
style crime!
wrong trainers

Fashion Girls get very concerned about things that no-one else would ever notice

Mumsy Girls

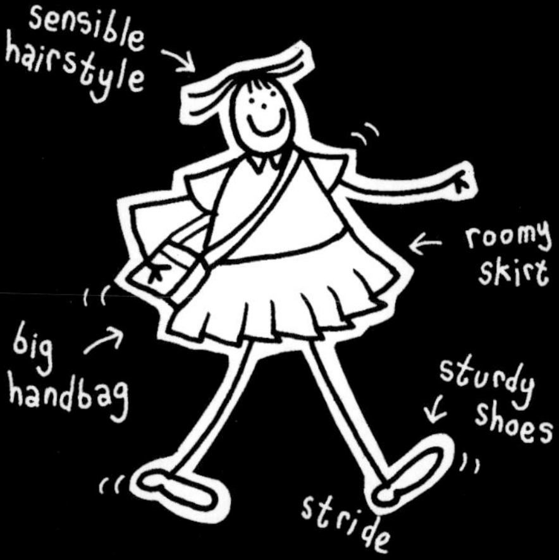

sensible hairstyle
roomy skirt
big handbag
sturdy shoes
stride

a poem about ↓

Mumsy Girls

It's best to avoid them
in public
Cos if you sneak off to
the lav
They shout at you
" please wipe your bottom
And don't come back here
till you have"

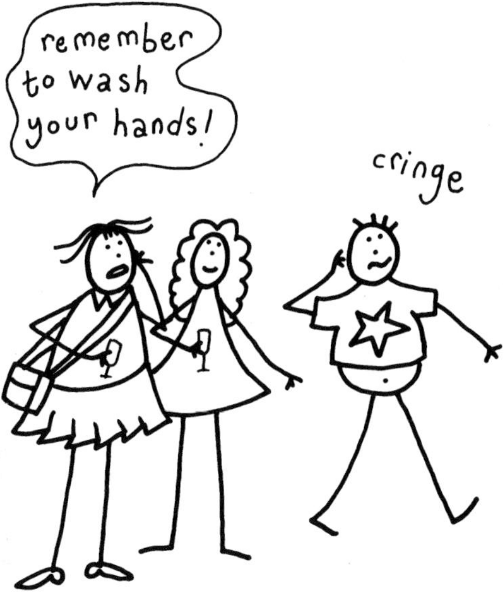
remember to wash your hands!
cringe

In private Mumsy Girls love to spank naughty little boys

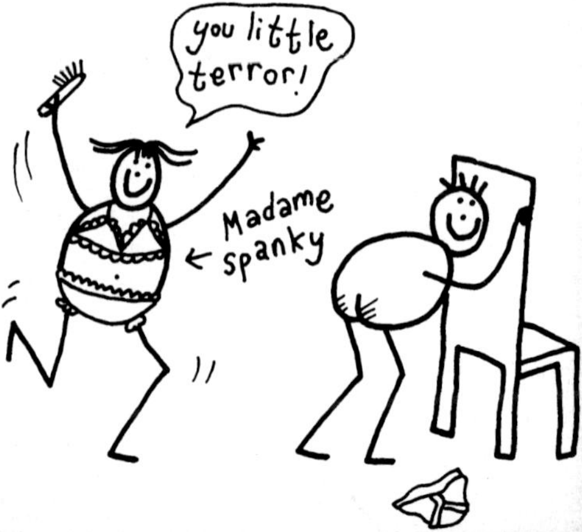
you little terror!
Madame spanky

Sporty Girls

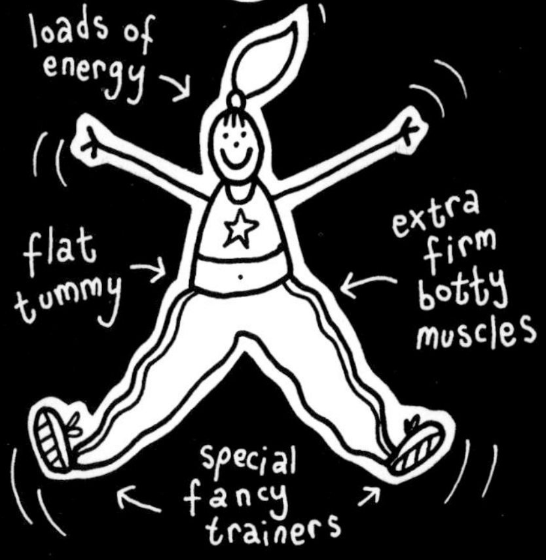

loads of energy
flat tummy
extra firm botty muscles
special fancy trainers

a poem about

Sporty Girls

It's best to tell a Sporty
Girl
That she's the one for you
Cos if you don't
She'll grab your wrist
And break you arm
in two

what am I?
deadly armlock
You're the most beautiful and lovely girl in the whole wide world ... ever

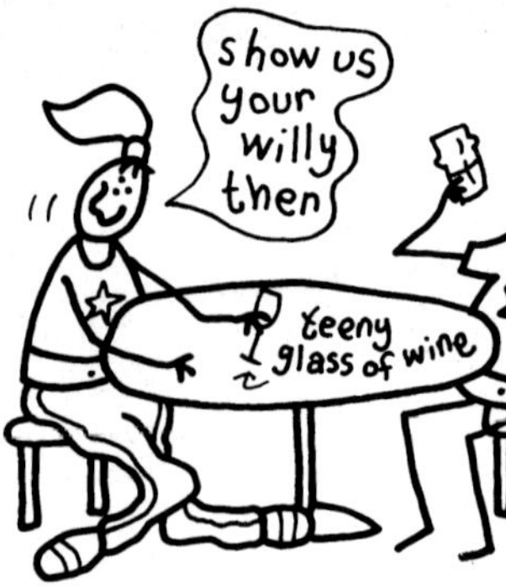
show us your willy then
teeny glass of wine

Sporty Girls are so fit that it usually only takes one drink to get them completely pissed

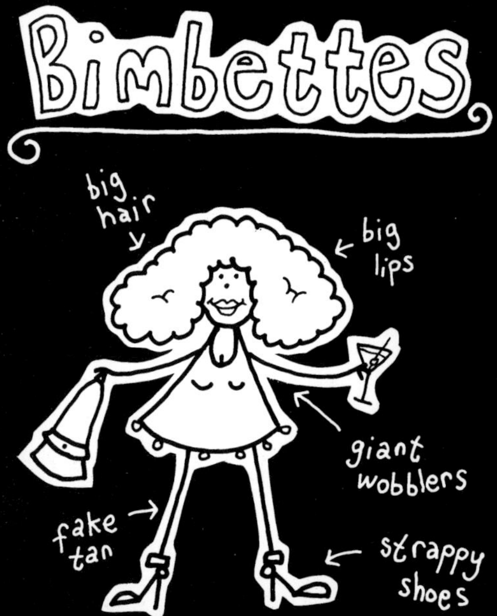
Bimbettes
big hair
big lips
giant wobblers
fake tan
strappy shoes

a poem about
↓

Bimbettes

They love to go shopping
together

And spend all the money
they have

At night they just dance
round their handbags

And laugh about boys in
the lav

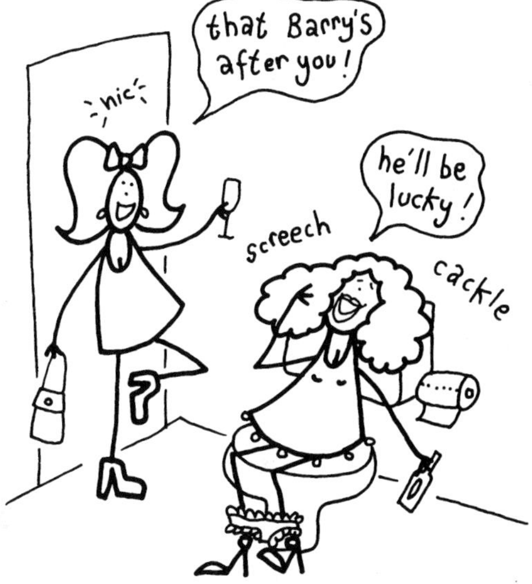
that Barry's after you!
hic
he'll be lucky!
screech
cackle

There is nothing a Bimbette loves more than a good night out with the girls

Perfect Girls

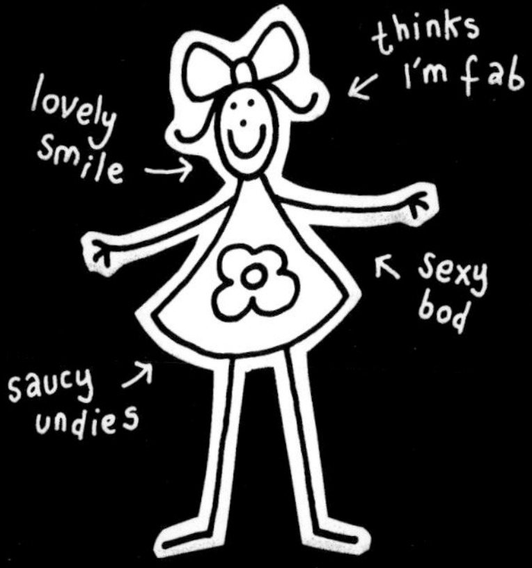
thinks I'm fab
lovely smile
sexy bod
saucy undies

a poem about
↓

Perfect Girls

You may think I'm being
soft-headed

You may think I'm being
a fool

But I would call any
girl perfect

Who tells me I'm sexy
and cool

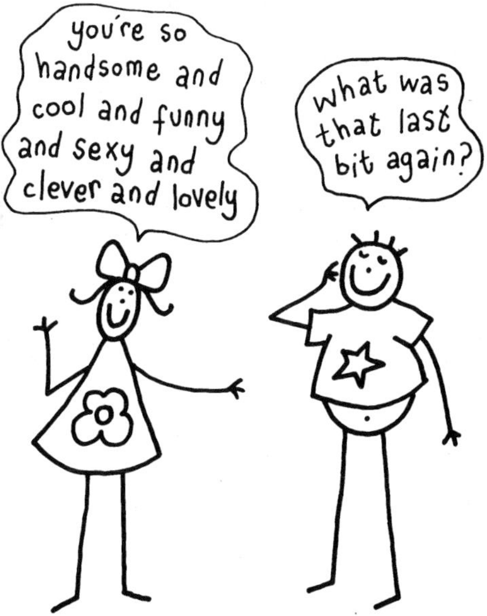
you're so handsome and cool and funny and sexy and clever and lovely
what was that last bit again?

When you take your clothes off for the first time a Perfect Girl knows exactly what to say

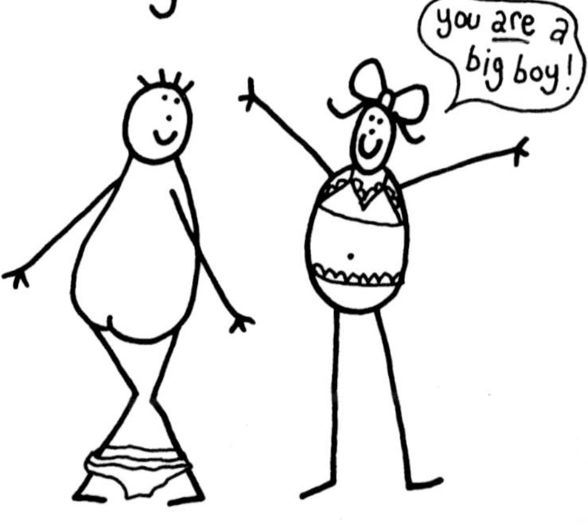
you are a big boy!